Published by Hodgson Consulting

© Copyright Hodgson Consulting 2012

The right of John Hodgson to be identified as the author of this work has been asserted in accordance with Section 77 of the Copyright, Designs and Patents Act 1988

All rights reserved. No part of this publication may be reproduced or transmitted in any form or by any means, electronic or mechanical, including photocopy, recording, or any information storage and retrieval system, without permission in writing from the publisher or copyright holder at:

8 Farm Rise, Whittlesford, Cambridge, CB22 4LZ, United Kingdom

ISBN 13-978-1475230116

Top Tips: Writing a CV/Résumé

INSTITUTE OF DIRECTORS

"The current job market is tougher than ever, with more talented people applying for fewer and fewer positions. Without a clear, focused and properly presented CV the chances of getting through to the next stage of the recruitment process is virtually impossible. **Top Tips: Writing a CV/Résumé** provides some very valuable insights that should not be ignored, After all, if *you* don't take your CV seriously, then employers won't either."

Ryan Ahern
Director of Learning and Development
Institute of Directors

Top Tips: Writing a CV/Résumé

by John Hodgson

Top Tips: Writing a CV/Résumé

CONTENTS

Introduction

1. ***Top Tips****: Preparation*

2. *Case Studies: 1986 and 2011*

3. *Formats*

4. *The Covering Letter*

5. ***Top Tips****: DO's and DON'Ts*

*Other **Top Tips** Titles*

About the Author

INTRODUCTION

The **Top Tips** series of mini books is a compendium of short, 20-30 minute reads.

Forty years of experience condensed into a series of 10 mini books. Each one takes less than 30 minutes to read and each one is a '*masterpiece of condensed learning*'.

A must for busy individuals who don't have the time to attend a training course on all 10 subjects covered in this unique series.

Is There a Difference Between a CV and a Résumé?

Curriculum Vitae is a Latin expression meaning 'the story of my life'. *Résumé* is a French word meaning: 'summary'. Think of *Curriculum Vitae* and *Résumé* as interchangeable terms – throughout this book we will use the abbreviation 'CV' to mean both.

Who Should Read This Book?

- ✓ Anybody contemplating applying for a job in the near future.
- ✓ Anybody thinking about dusting off and updating an old CV.
- ✓ Anybody who has submitted a CV and is still waiting for a response.

Your CV is the key that will open the door to the interview room. If it doesn't fit you will remain on the outside.

Top Tips: Writing a CV/Résumé

At this stage don't get too concerned about the interview. In fact, don't even think about it. The overriding objective is to own a CV which **stands out from the crowd** and gets placed on the pile marked: 'for interview'.

Look at it this way: you are already one step ahead of the competition simply by taking the time to read this book.

- ✓ Be happy. You're on the way.

What Will You Learn From Reading This Book?

If you have expectations of being interviewed in the near future and would like to improve your chances of being offered the job, you will most certainly benefit from reading this book. You will learn:

- ✓ Why a high percentage of CVs get **scanned** but not **read**.
- ✓ How to write a winning CV.
- ✓ How to engage the reader in **10 seconds**.

You will also learn:

- ✓ How to read a job advertisement.
- ✓ How to **tune in** to the needs of the employer and **match** your CV to the job offer.
- ✓ The Do's and Don'ts when submitting a CV.
- ✓ The secrets of a strong covering letter.

The Interview

To avoid confusion, this book contains **Top Tips** on the CV and covering letter alone. It does not contain tips on how best to approach the interview. These can be found in a separate 30 minute mini book – ***Top Tips: Interviewing***.

Confession:

I cannot claim all the credit for what you're about to read. I am fortunate to be able to directly approach employers and other experts around the world to get current thinking on the attributes of an outstanding CV. They've told me what they like and dislike, what works and doesn't work, and they passed on tips on **preparation** and **presentation**.

Top Tips: Writing a CV/Résumé

CONTENT

You must help the recruiter form a mental picture of you and enable them to match **their needs** with **your skills and experience**.

Your CV **must** include:

- ✓ Your name, address and contact details.
- ✓ A brief **summary of achievements** in bullet form.
- ✓ Work experience including current position and responsibilities.
- ✓ Key skills.
- ✓ Employment history.
- ✓ Education and qualifications.
- ✓ Interests and hobbies.

Let's test the water with a short exercise.

Below, you will see an advertisement for a vacancy for Head of Sales and Marketing. After studying it, I'd like you to take a blank sheet of paper or use the NOTES pages at the back of this book, and list the **key words** which describe the job and what skills you believe the advertiser is seeking.

SAMPLE ADVERTISEMENT:

Head of Sales and Marketing
Central London. Salary: circa £60,000 ($95,000)

Our client is a leading provider of training and requires an experienced manager to lead a team of salespeople and to run the sales and marketing department. You will work closely with the General Manager and senior management team.

You will be responsible for building marketing and sales strategies across all channels, including advertising, direct marketing and web marketing.

The successful applicant must be able to demonstrate continued learning and development within sales and marketing.

Previous experience must include managing a sales team through effective and proven management practice.

Please forward your CV to jobloggs@abcrecruitment.org

ABC Recruitment will only respond to successful applicants.

Top Tips: Writing a CV/Résumé

The key words or phrases that you should have identified are:

SAMPLE ADVERTISEMENT:

Head of Sales and Marketing
Central London. Salary: circa £60,000 ($95,000)

Our **client** is a **leading provider** of **training** and requires an **experienced manager** to **lead a team** of **salespeople** and to run the **sales and marketing department**. You will work closely with the General Manager and senior management team.

You will be **responsible** for building **marketing and sales strategies** across **all channels**, including **advertising, direct marketing and web marketing**.

The successful applicant must be able to **demonstrate continued learning and development** within sales and marketing.

Previous experience must include managing a sales team through effective and proven management practice.

Please forward your CV to jobloggs@abcrecruitment.org

ABC Recruitment will only respond to successful applicants.

First of all, if your list is slightly different, do not fret – it's nothing to get concerned about. The whole purpose of the exercise is to draw attention to the need to **read the advertisement with care**. It is the first step in matching their needs with your skills and experience. These words will enable you to **tune in** to the express **needs** of the employer.

Other key points you should have noticed:

- The name of the employer is not mentioned.

- The job location is not mentioned.

- ABC Recruitment has been hired to place the advertisement and draw up a shortlist of candidates.

- The advertisement calls for an online response: this is **critical** information. Your CV will be viewed on a screen and may only be printed to verify the number of responses the advertisement generated.

- Only when you click on 'submit' will you know if you have to complete an online application form or be invited to submit a pre-prepared CV.

- The ad states that only successful applicants will receive a response. In which case, you will never know how close you were to being invited to interview or why you failed to get on the list. It could be that it had nothing to do with presentation but that other candidates were better qualified.

Your CV may well have reached column three of the graph below and been studied in detail but you will never know.

Research reveals:

ALL CVs will be **scanned** – relatively few will actually be **read**.

- 30-40% CVs may be rejected on sight.

- Less than 10% will be studied thoroughly.

- 5% of applicants may be invited to an interview.

- ONE person will get the job.

Top Tips: Writing a CV/Résumé

Providing that you follow the guidelines for simple formatting and **highlighting** contained in this book, the chance of having your CV properly examined will increase dramatically.

✓ Your CV must have instant appeal.

The following bar chart shows what typically happens when 100 applicants chase a single vacancy.

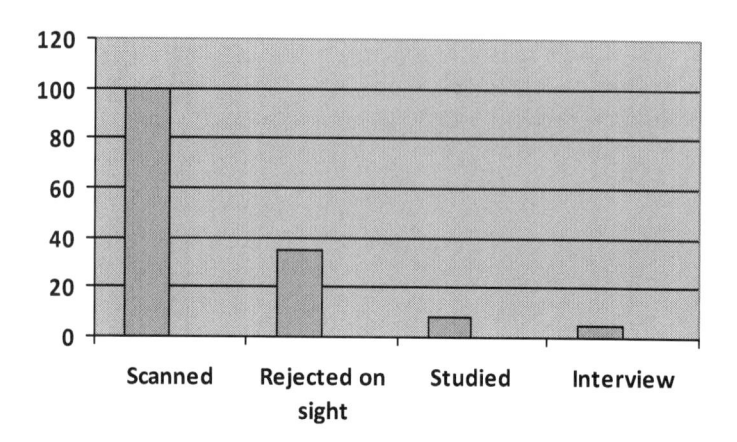

[Bar chart: Scanned ≈ 100, Rejected on sight ≈ 35, Studied ≈ 7, Interview ≈ 3]

The tall column on the left represents the number of CVs submitted for a single vacancy, in this case, 100. However, if the current economic climate prevails, don't be surprised to see this number rise. You may find yourself competing against **200-300 applicants** for a **single vacancy**.

The second column (from left to right) represents the percentage of CVs that may be **rejected on sight**! 30-40% is not uncommon.

Column three shows that we're now down to less than 10% of the original number. This is the percentage of CVs which **will** be studied or read.

The fourth and final column represents the percentage of applicants who will be invited to attend an interview. Thus, **95% of ALL applicants** can expect to receive a letter containing the words: *'we regret to say that on this occasion you have not been successful...we will keep your letter/application on file....'*

Many candidates will remain blissfully unaware that they never gave themselves a fair chance. It would be a brave employer who replied: *'You know what? Nobody bothered to read your CV because it looked terrible.'*

Reading a CV

A CV is read differently to most other textual documents. Unlike a book or a letter, a CV needs to be **written in direct language** which can be **scanned quickly for meaning**.

A powerful CV is not dissimilar to a professionally written job description. A job description begins with a job title followed by a brief summary of duties.

KEY POINTS:

- ✓ The summary is **read** first.
- ✓ The rest of the document is then **scanned** quickly for job titles, bullet statements and other highlighted material.
- ✓ Research suggests that you have **10 seconds** to grab attention and encourage the reader to engage.
- ✓ If they do read on, you have **45 seconds** to sell yourself.

General Principles:

- Employers are only generally interested in the last 10-15 years of experience because that is all that is relevant to the challenges they face today.
- ✗ Avoid placing too much emphasis on hobbies/interests unless helpful in determining your ability to do the job.
- ✗ Do not use a standard template downloaded from the internet. If your CV looks like dozens of others, you may be considered lazy. Not a good start.

- ✗ Do not use the phrase: '*I work well both on my own and in a team*'. It is a pet hate of many employers and can be summed up by this contribution from a leading employer: '*I hate to see those dreaded words. It's hard to find a more trite sentence that adds no value whatsoever!*'

- ✓ Your CV needs to be **eye-catching** and convey an instant impression of a caring professional.

Top Tips: Writing a CV/Résumé

Electronic Screening

An increasing number of employers are turning to digital scanning of CVs.

For example, let's say a bank receives 4,000 applications. (I'll wait while you read that again.) Yes, 4,000 applications for 40 vacancies. In this case, they may use an electronic scanner which will be programmed to **detect key words**.

Top Tip: Scanners <u>do not like underlining</u> so, if you want a word or phrase to stand out, make sure it is in **bold** and not <u>underlined.</u>

This is yet another reason to read the advertisement carefully and pick out the key words so that the **screening process** will **identify** you as a potential candidate.

- ✓ Make sure you include the most important words from the advert in your CV or covering letter.

Students

If you are a student then you won't need reminding that elite universities have raised the bar on entrance qualifications. What was acceptable a few years ago is no longer good enough. Universities expect to be able to choose from candidates with a string of A*s. Similarly, when you leave university or college, merely having a degree won't make you **stand out**.

However, universities and employers **will** be impressed if you can provide **evidence** of qualities gained from an **extra curricula activity**.

In the UK, the *Duke of Edinburgh Award Scheme* is recognised as an organisation that equips young people with skills that are **transferrable** to the workplace.

In the United States, the *Youth Service of America* is one of the many organisations that prepares the youth of today for the challenges of tomorrow.

In fact, right across the world young people have opportunities to give up their time to the benefit of the community and themselves, so:

- ✗ Do not fall into the trap of thinking that what you do in your spare time is not important. It *is* important and can make the difference between being invited to interview or not.

Think of yourself as a product

- ✓ Your product needs to have immediate appeal to a potential buyer.
- ✓ You need to create a desire for them to want to know more about you.

Top Tips: Writing a CV/Résumé

Have you already searched the web?

I'd be surprised if you haven't. Chances are that, like me, you have discovered a mind-boggling number of sites offering thousands of "individuals" the *ultimate* CV.

There is, however, **no way** that you'll come across as an individual and stand out from the crowd if you simply join the masses who are looking for a quick-fix CV and expect to have everything done for them.

✓ Make sure that you don't come across as a clone.

Prices for a downloadable CV fall in a price range of £25-£500 ($39-$775). So, what do you get for your money? Let's see. Here's what I found:

- Recruitment agencies offering the world. No guarantees but then, none expected.

- You may be presented with a three-tier price structure. You may be asked to enter your credit card details and choose from a price list which reflects the division of time and effort invested. That is: between *your* time and *their* time: the less you do, the more you'll pay and that's only fair.

- The price list may be a simple price per page with a tempting low price to draw you in. Very soon you'll find that your CV won't fit neatly on a single page. Now there's a surprise, but the good news is, it looks perfect when spread over two pages!

- Be careful that you're not signing up for a monthly fee. Why would you need an ongoing subscription?

Typical three-tier price structure:

Introductory CV: You write it. They'll rewrite it and charge you for the privilege.

Intermediate: For positions with a salary between £20,000-£49,000 ($31,000-$75,000) – expect to pay between £50-£199 ($77-$310).

Premium: Carries a premium price. This will be a bespoke CV/Résumé. If you're willing to spend £500-£800 ($775-$1,240) to have third party write your CV, I do wonder who else might regard that as a questionable business decision. On the other hand, if you can afford it and genuinely believe that it will open doors for you – go for it.

For very senior appointments with a salary above £150,000 ($230,000) you may well decide that the premium service is a wise investment. At this level your CV must be **flawless**. Attention to detail is paramount and there is no room for mistakes.

Should you waiver over the price, you may be offered the 'covering letter' at an all-inclusive price to save £50 ($75). This is known as a 'special opportunity close' and you will be asked to enter your credit card details within a limited time frame to qualify.

We've already established that there's every possibility that you have searched the internet for options, so you don't need me to tell you that "free downloads" come at a price.

Nothing comes free. In terms of value for money, *Top Tips: Writing a CV/Résumé* is probably as close as it gets. You have all this for less than £5 ($7).

Top Tips: Writing a CV/Résumé

TOP TIPS: PREPARATION

Let's get started…

Preparation means doing your homework. There are no shortcuts. If you want the job of your dreams, you need to invest a little time.

You've already carried out an exercise to identify key words in an advertisement. Now study the following advertisement and imagine it's one you saw on the internet:

> Marketing and Communications Officer
> Edinburgh
> Maxwall Housing Association
> Registered Charity Number 567123
> Permanent. Salary: £32,000 ($49,000)
> Job Ref: 13214904
>
> This exciting role is to set up the Marketing and Communications function within Maxwall Housing Association, the largest part of the Glencoe Housing Group.
>
> Based in impressive new HQ in Edinburgh this position is an excellent opportunity for you to make a positive impact in social housing and promote Maxwall throughout Scotland.
>
> You will lead and develop marketing and communications strategies for the group through integrated channels and through customer-focused and effective communications services.

> You will be responsible for the development of Maxwall Housing Association's external reputation through marketing and public relations activity surrounding marketing campaigns and events.
>
> This role requires blue sky thinking and innovation to expand accessibility to the Association's websites and through social media and blogs.
>
> The day-to-day responsibilities include sourcing stories and writing copy for internal and external publications, managing the website and liaising with the media to implement public relations campaigns alongside marketing strategies and promotional events.

Note: This exercise is a test of reading and understanding the advertisement.

- *You should have noticed that the company is part of the Glencoe Group.*

- *Did you notice that the company is a registered charity?*

- *Is it right to assume that the parent company is also a charity?*

- *How can you find out more about housing associations?*

- *Take a blank sheet of paper and make a list of the **key words** so that you will be **tuned in** to the critical needs.*

- *What might you be expected to take to the interview? eg. if you were applying for a position as a graphic artist, designer, sign writer or photographer, you'd be expected to show evidence of your work.*

- *In the example, 'writing copy' will be a daily responsibility. What do you have that will impress?*

Top Tips: Writing a CV/Résumé

- *How does the company spell its name? Maxwell or Maxwall?* I once worked for a manufacturing company that produced old-fashioned consumer products (at the time we thought they were state-of-the-art because they used transistors!) The brand name was EKCO, named after the founder Mr. Eric K Cole. Any applicant who addressed his/her letter to ECKO or, would you believe, ECHO, didn't get off to a very good start. You may be wondering why we saw them at all. Simple. If we ruled out the people who got it wrong, we wouldn't have had anyone to see.

Although you're not at the interview stage yet, you need to start thinking about these things right from the start to avoid being embarrassed.

Where to find information about the organisation you hope to join

- ✓ Develop a strategy to learn as much about the company and industry as you can.
- ✓ Start with the advertisement. Look for a reference to a **parent** or **subsidiary** company.
- ✓ Go to their **website**.

Play detective and gather evidence. The moment you decide to apply to an advertisement is the moment you start gathering information:

- Who are they?
- Where have they been?
- Where are they heading?

The advertisement may list **specific skills** or **experience** that the successful applicant will need to be able to demonstrate.

Every industry has a trade magazine or trade newspaper:

- ✓ Find out what it is and get the latest edition. You may discover other openings within the same organisation.
- ✓ Get a copy of the company's Annual Report and Accounts.

Annual Report and Accounts

If the company is listed on the stock exchange, this information will be in the public domain and simple to attain. Call the company secretary's office or go online and download a copy.

Top Tips: Writing a CV/Résumé

In the UK, all limited liability companies will have Ltd or Limited after their name and they must, by law, file their annual accounts at Companies House. For a modest sum, you will be able to download the accounts to your computer.

Don't be intimidated if you don't know how to read a Profit and Loss Account or Balance Sheet. The Annual Report and Accounts could still prove to be your most valuable asset. Typically, the report will begin with a statement from the Chairman or CEO. This statement will tell you all that you need to know about where the company has come from (last year's lows and highs) and its vision of the future. This will be followed by reports from senior operating officers.

- ✓ Look for the company's *Mission Statement* and *Vision Statement*, should they have one.

- ✓ Consider the recruiting company that has been hired to do the interviewing. Read their publications and current areas of investigation.

- ✓ Consider the newspaper carrying the ad. From this you can deduce the readership and the cost: a national publication will cost more to advertise in and will be aimed to reach more people than a small ad in a local newspaper. It may indicate that the company is willing to contribute to relocation costs.

Are There Times When a CV is Considered Unnecessary?

Yes. There are departments within the civil service and government departments where you will be expected to complete one of their own application forms. If so:

- ✗ Do not ignore the request.
- ✗ Do not submit your own CV.

The person at the other end will be forced to search through your CV to find what they're looking for. They won't like that. They might think – and rightly so, in my view – that if you can't be bothered to fill in their application form, why should they bother to wade through your CV?

Photographs

- ✗ Do not include a photo unless relevant to the job.

It is more important to spend time on your CV to make sure that you bring out the relevant aspects of your experience to match the job advertised.

- ✓ Apply some lateral thinking.

Lateral thinking

You may be applying for a job where tact and diplomacy are required. If you've had work experience in a restaurant or bar it might be seen as experience of having to think on your feet, work long hours and with discretion.

Top Tips: Writing a CV/Résumé

Is it possible for one format to be successful over a period of 25 years?

The answer here is an emphatic 'YES'.

I can hear gasps of surprise from recruitment agencies but the fact is that I have used a basic **format** for CVs spanning a period of 25 years – with a 100% success record.

I deliberately chose the word 'format'. I am not suggesting that one CV will be effective on all occasions. If you were to apply for two different jobs in the same industry, you would need to **adapt your CV to meet the express needs of each employer.**

It is the **format** not the **content** that worked successfully in the years between 1986 and 2011.

You will shortly see how the **summary of achievements** is made to stand out. It is designed to be **eye-catching**. It is clean and simple and gets straight to the point. The format draws you in. It's impossible to ignore.

If you've already read *Top Tips: Interviewing* you'll know that at the time of writing it I had one assumption: that the reader already owned a CV and was seeking advice before attending an interview.

In this book my assumption is that you are contemplating applying for a job or considering a career change and looking for ideas and guidance. You may have received one of those dreaded letters of rejection and are looking for help and advice on how to get your first interview.

- No matter how qualified you are, without the right CV you will not get an interview. Put another way, a poorly presented CV may be binned before it's even read.

- The compelling reason for writing this book is that most people get their CV wrong.

- As you discover the secrets of writing a successful CV you'll realise that there **are no secrets!** Just common sense.

- The good news is that when you hold your new CV in your hand your confidence will receive a boost and so too will your earning potential.

- **Remember: you have 10 seconds to make an impact and 45 seconds to sell yourself.**

Top Tips: Writing a CV/Résumé

CASE STUDIES: 1986 AND 2011

Case Study One: 1986

The year is 1986. I was a tutor on a two day open workshop about personal development called *Thinking For Success*.

One of the participants was a professional headhunter. He explained his role as that of a professional middle man: he was employed by an organisation to screen applicants and their applications and put forward a shortlist of names to be interviewed. Only when the position was filled would he earn his commission. He explained that it was not uncommon to arrive at the office and come face-to-face with 200-300 applications for a single vacancy.

He jokingly said he would divide the large pile of CVs into two smaller ones and throw one pile in the bin. '*Those guys are unlucky!*' he said, adding: '*who would want to employ somebody who is that unlucky?*'

To be serious, reading through so many applications is a daunting prospect and a large percentage of CVs left him feeling angry. As he put it: '*You wouldn't believe some of the letters and CVs I get,* (expletive deleted) *a surprisingly high number of candidates get it so wrong and then wonder why they're not invited to attend an interview*'.

1986 was the year I met the head hunter. 1986 was the year I first appreciated the door-opening properties of a **well-constructed** and **well-presented** CV. At the time my son was embarking on his career and I'd helped him put his first CV together. Proudly, I showed it to my new friend the head hunter. He was polite and, luckily for me, was enjoying the course. He offered to take it away and lay it out in a format that would convey the key points within 10 seconds, adding: '*I promise not to change the content. Just rearrange it*'.

A week later, my son posted four CVs in the newly suggested format. He was invited to four interviews and received two job offers. He was on his way to a successful career in the pharmaceutical industry.

Top Tips: Writing a CV/Résumé

Case Study Two: 2011

Now fast forward to the summer of 2011. Names of people and places have been changed to preserve anonymity.

I was involved in organising a charity golf day for a local hospice. 120 golfers took part one glorious day in June. The event raised £6,060 ($9,500) for the *Arthur Rank Hospice Charity* and one of the players won a set of *Callaway* golf clubs for achieving a hole-in-one. A great day for everybody involved.

Two days later a lady in our village asked me how the day went. She quickly added that her son was an apprentice green keeper at the golf club and had been up at 4:30am every day for two weeks to make sure the course was in tip top condition. I was able to tell her that she had every reason to be proud of him: almost every player had commented on the course and had been heaping praise on the club captain, much to his delight.

The apprentice was a 19 year old lad who was proud of his work but had his sights set on working for a more prestigious golf club in Cambridgeshire, England. When his mother said he was planning to submit his CV, I asked her if I could see it.

It contained the same classic mistakes which the head hunter had pointed out 25 years earlier:

- ✗ It was too long.
- ✗ Chronologically, it was back-to-front.
- ✗ No list of achievements.
- ✗ Most recent work experience was on the second page.
- ✗ No highlights. No attention-grabbing headlines.
- ✗ Reading it was hard work.

It was destined for the round filing bin on the floor. Here's what we did:

I began by asking him to write a list of his responsibilities at work. He went away and came back with the following:

My responsibilities at work:

Greens mowing, tees mowing, fairway mowing, semi-rough mowing, long-rough mowing, bunker raking and maintenance, changing holes, irrigation operation and repairs, tree planting, fertilising, over seed and top dressing, machine maintenance and repairs.

Now let's look at how we put this into his CV.

Top Tips: Writing a CV/Résumé

JOHN FREEMAN
CURRICULUM VITAE

Date of birth: 19th April 1990
Address: 1204, Honeywell Lane
Jackson
Essex ES3 4NJ
Tel: 01234 567890

Brief summary of achievements:
- Assistant Green Keeper – East Anglia Golf Club, 2011
- Outstanding Student award 2010 – Williams Agricultural College
- Team Leader – Trans-Africa Expedition, 2009
- Studying for a diploma in Sports Turf Management

Current responsibilities:
Greens mowing
Tees mowing
Fairway mowing
Semi-rough and long-rough mowing
Bunker raking and maintenance
Changing holes
Irrigation operation and repairs
Tree planting
Fertilising
Over seed and top dressing
Machine maintenance and repair

Education: Turnberry College
Science (A)
Maths (B)
English (A*)
College of East Anglia
Resistant Materials Technology (A*)
Parts 1 – 6 Spraying Certificate

St John's First Aid Certificate – pass with distinction

At 19 and with limited experience it was possible to put everything on a single sheet of paper. John Freeman attached a covering letter to his CV and addressed it to the General Manager of the aforementioned prestigious golf club.

A week later he was invited to attend an interview. One week after the interview he was offered the job.

January 2012: he goes to work with a smile on his face. He has the job of his dreams.

This is a true story and the amazing thing is that there was **no advertisement** because there was no vacancy! Members of the committee were so impressed with his **initiative** and enthusiasm that they created a vacancy for him.

Observations:

Notice how the **brief** summary of achievements painted a word picture of John. With four bullet points he demonstrated determination, relevant experience and other admirable qualities.

References:

You may wonder why there was no line that said: *'References available on request'*.

This statement is superfluous. It's merely stating the obvious: the time to deal with references is when you're called for the interview.

Now let's look at another CV which uses the same format for a more senior position.

Top Tips: Writing a CV/Résumé

DENISE REACHER
RETAIL BUSINESS CONSULTANT

123 High Street
Middle Common
Maidenhead
Berks BLT 45

Tel: 044 234 5678
Mobile: 07999 112 112
Email: denise.r@hotmail.co.uk

Summary of achievements:
- Business Woman of the Month, Sept 2011 – Young Style Magazine
- Regional Manager for 80 retail outlets – ABC Fashion
- Achieved success in restructuring inter-company distribution network.
- Added new lines and £3m/$4.6m profit before tax, 2010

Current responsibilities:
Editor – Teen Fashion

Core competencies:
Communication – managed an integrated, company-wide incentive scheme
Financial awareness – IoD Chartered Director Diploma

Note: In Denise's case she decided that at this level there would be no need to put 'Curriculum Vitae' at the top as it is self-evident. She used the line to communicate another message.

And here's an extract from the advertisement:

> *Leading nationwide fashion retailer looking for dynamic individual for position as Marketing Director.*
> *Must have good communication skills and retail experience with a large chain.*

You don't need to see any more of her CV to know she will get an interview and, unless she's been stretching the truth, she will probably get the job.

Honesty:

If you are not **completely honest** about your experience and achievements you **will** be found out.

Address and contact details:

There are people who will tell you that personal details and address should be placed at the foot of the document so that the first vital seconds are maximised and used to convey crucial and relevant personal strengths. Here are some guidelines:

- If you believe there will be **multiple applications**, put your contact and address details at the **top** of the CV.

- When applying for a **middle management position**, put the contact and address details at the **foot** of the CV so that your job-related strengths and summary of achievements give maximum impact.

- If the role you're applying for is **internal** your details will already be known so it's perfectly acceptable to put them at the **foot**.

Top Tips: Writing a CV/Résumé

Dates:

What is noticeable about these four dates?

- 5th September 2012
- September 5th 2012
- 5/9/12
- 9/5/12

They're all the same: one date presented in four different ways. I strongly recommend that you adopt the style: **5th September 2012** for your CV and covering letter. **Never** use numbers alone. Here's why:

Invite one American and one European to an event held on 5/9/12. The America will arrive on 9th May 2012 and European will arrive five months later on 5th September 2012. Confusion arises because in different parts of the world the format is MM:DD:YEAR whilst in others it is DD:MM:YEAR.

I am not prepared to say how I discovered this, other than to say that it's based on an embarrassing personal experience as a newly appointed Export Manager.

THE COVERING LETTER

Despite what others might tell you, a CV should **never** be submitted **without** a covering letter.

As we've already established, your CV needs to be presented in an attention-grabbing way because some are only scanned, whereas your covering letter is most likely to be **read in full**.

This gives you a fantastic **opportunity** to encourage the reader to **want** to read your CV. Just as your CV needs to be **tailored** to the specific job, so does your covering letter.

Your covering letter must **complement** your CV. It should contain:

- ✓ An **introduction** – your name and the position you are applying for, including the appropriate reference number for the advertisement/job.

- ✓ A **brief explanation** of why your experience may **differentiate** you from other candidates. The right covering letter should encourage the reader to pay special attention to your CV.

- ✓ If requested to send it by email, always send the covering letter as an attachment.

Disclosure of disability:

You are not legally bound to declare a disability on your CV or in your covering letter. However, failure to do so on an application form or medical form, when specifically asked, may lead to problems down the line – including dismissal.

Top Tips: Writing a CV/Résumé

If you do decide to disclose, stress your positive attributes and outline the benefits of your disability: outline the extra skills you have gained as a result of your disability. You could use your covering letter to give examples of how you have successfully dealt with challenges in the past brought on by your disability.

TOP TIPS: DO'S AND DON'TS

DO's

- Do **read and re-read the advertisement** to make sure you've not overlooked something vital. eg. If you're asked to complete the company's own application form and not a CV, do as requested.

- Do make sure your CV is **tailored** to match the job specification.

- Do check the **cut-off date** and make certain that you submit your application in good time.

- Do ask somebody to read through your application and covering letter for **spelling** and **grammar errors**. (Research suggests that 70% of CVs contain errors.)

- Do keep a copy of your CV by the telephone in case you get a **screening call**. You may be asked questions about what you've written and you need to have all the facts at your fingertips.

- Do check to see where the job is located. Just because the head office is in New York or London does not mean that that's where you'll be based.

- Do check with the people you've listed as **referees** that you have their permission to include their name and contact details.

- Do look at your CV as if it were an advertisement. Does it pass the **10 second test**?

- Do remember: the summary is **read first**. The rest of the document will be **scanned** quickly for **job titles**, **bullet points** and other **highlighted** material.

Top Tips: Writing a CV/Résumé

✓ Do, if you have time, **post** your application and CV to **yourself**. When the letter arrives you'll open it and quickly see exactly what your intended recipient will see. Don't be surprised if you decide to make a last minute change.

DON'T's

✗ **Don't send a general purpose CV**. There is nothing more annoying than for an employer to receive a CV which has clearly been sent to dozens of other companies with no attempt at tailoring.

✗ Don't post your CV without having first checked it for typos and grammar errors by another person.

✗ Don't rely on **spellcheck**. eg. Compliment/complement, principle/principal, formerly/formally and other such telling errors suggest that you might send out something embarrassing for the new company.

✗ Don't guess the postage. Companies don't like having to pay excess postage on anything, let alone a job application.

✗ Don't use an envelope with your current company logo on it.

✗ Don't post your letter from your current employer's post room with a franked/printed stamp on it.

✗ Don't show your keyboard creativity with a variety of fonts, colours and sound clips.

✗ Don't skimp on the **time** you spend writing your CV. It will be a false economy.

✗ Don't put forward names of parents as referees if all that they're able to confirm is that you are an honest, trustworthy and reliable babysitter – particularly if you're 30!

- ✗ Don't use photocopy paper or a brown envelope.

- ✗ Don't send it without first sending it to yourself as an email attachment so that you can see how it appears on-screen. A prospective employer may wish to forward it to other interested parties.

- ✗ Don't leave that 'highly amusing' message on your answering machine.

- ✗ Don't forget to check that the font used in the covering letter matches the one in your CV.

Thank you for reading ***Top Tips: Writing a CV/Résumé***. I wish you well in your career and sincerely hope that you have found your investment in this book to have been worthwhile.

Top Tips: Writing a CV/Résumé

OTHER TOP TIPS TITLES

Top Tips: Interviewing

Top Tips: Selling

Top Tips: Negotiating

Top Tips: Goal Setting

Top Tips: Communication

Top Tips: Time Management

Top Tips: Creative Thinking

Top Tips: Problem Solving

Top Tips: Effective Delegation

About The Author

John Hodgson is widely known as a successful businessman and business consultant.

He has 20 years of experience working with *Philips Consumer Products* in the UK and Overseas.

He was Managing Director of *Mandev Training*, *Gooding International* and a board member of *Race Electronics*.

He was a founder of *RH International* and *OEM Services* with offices in the USA, Hong Kong, Taiwan and a joint venture in Xiamen, China.

John has spent 10 years as a senior lecturer at the *Institute of Directors* and worked with hundreds of individuals representing a diverse group of blue chip organisations.

Author of *Test Your Financial Awareness* published by Hodder & Stoughton and **Top Tips: Interviewing** also available from Amazon.

Top Tips: Writing a CV/Résumé

ACKNOWLEDGEMENTS

My grateful thanks must go to the following people, without whom this book might never have been written. Their wisdom, support and advice is much appreciated:

Charlotte Choules

Annie Clarke

Frank Clarke

Kevin Hempson

Christina Hughes

Dr Lynn Morgan

Dr Samantha Rayner

Terry Riley

Jack Sutcliffe

Graeme Udall

WITH SPECIAL THANKS TO

Anglia Ruskin University

Cambridge, England

Charlotte Choules is studying the post-graduate MA Publishing course at Anglia Ruskin University, Cambridge, 2011/2012.

She has shown real initiative and enthusiasm for her career in publishing by volunteering to help with the design, formatting, editing and proof-reading of this book and the *Top Tips* series.

The end result is testament to the course and tutors.

My thanks also to Anglia Ruskin University for allowing and, indeed, encouraging her participation.

For information on the course go to:
www.anglia.ac.uk/ruskin/en/home.html

Top Tips: Writing a CV/Résumé

Notes

Notes

Top Tips: Writing a CV/Résumé

Notes